You Will Receive Power

You Will Receive Power

The Holy Spirit and His Gifts

Ian Petit OSB

Illustrated by
Elizabeth Ruth Obbard

DARTON·LONGMAN + TODD

First published in 1994 by
Darton, Longman and Todd Ltd
1 Spencer Court
140-142 Wandsworth High Street
London SW18 4JJ

Reprinted 1998

ISBN 0–232–52090–9

A catalogue record for this book is available
from the British Library

The Scripture quotations in this publication are taken from *The
Jerusalem Bible* published and copyright 1966, 1967 and 1968 by
Darton, Longman and Todd Ltd and Doubleday and Co. Inc.

Phototypeset by Intype, London
Printed and bound in Great Britain by
Redwood Books, Trowbridge, Wiltshire

Contents

Contents

Introduction

I grew up not knowing very much about the Holy Spirit. In those days we called him Holy Ghost, and that was not very helpful. When I became a monk and priest much of my studies were spent considering the Father and the Son – we did not devote a great deal of time to the Spirit in those days.

However, towards the latter part of this century, there has been a renewed interest in the Holy Spirit, much of it caused by the Pentecostal Movement. This movement, which sprang from the Pentecostal Church and entered the main-line Protestant Churches in the 1950s and the Roman Catholic Church in the 1960s, emphasises the power of the Holy Spirit manifested chiefly in the charismatic gifts or gifts of the Spirit.

I became involved in this renewal and my first real encounter with the Holy Spirit was through the charisms, the power gifts. Up till then much of my understanding of the gospel message had been concentrated on dying to self, carrying one's cross, being brave under trial. Suddenly I was discovering a whole new side to the gospel – the Lord in rising had conquered and we in his name were sent out to minister his victory to the broken-hearted, the lame, the sick. We were not called to carry every cross and offer up every trial: we were to minister the Lord's victory and set people free. It was heady stuff.

It seems amazing to me that I could have missed this side of the gospel and concentrated on the dying to self, the brave embracing of hardships; but when you do not read the whole gospel and just confine yourself to what the Sunday readings give, then I suppose it is not surprising if you end up with an impoverished understanding.

The next lesson I had to learn was not to jettison the suffering-cross side of the gospel but to learn to live in this strange land where 'all has-been-achieved' and yet somehow 'is-not-yet-achieved' in us. Both themes are in the one gospel and it is neither victory all the way nor suffering and pain all the way – strange bedfellows indeed.

When I was asked to write this book it was intended to be on the gifts of the Holy Spirit, but the more I worked on it the more I realised that that would emphasise the power side of the gospel and thus give a lopsided view of the Holy Spirit's work. He has come to do far more than just give us charismatic gifts.

I believe that there are two sorts of empowering that the Spirit does. One is personal and is concerned with making all that Jesus has achieved for us effective in us. Jesus came to put our Adam life to death and give us a share in his risen, new life. In the fourth eucharistic prayer we say: 'That we might no longer live for ourselves but for him, he sent the Holy Spirit from you, Father, as his first gift to those who believe, to complete his work on earth and bring us the fulness of grace.' This clearly expresses the first work of the Holy Spirit, which empowers us to live a new life on the condition that we let go of the old. There is the rub. We have constantly to let go of the old life applying the Cross of Jesus, and to rise to new life with him. This does not just happen; our task is to allow God to make it happen, and he acts when we have faith in what Jesus has done. So this first empowering of the Spirit has much to do with sacrifice, self-surrender, and death.

The other empowering is the gifting with spiritual power gifts or charisms. These gifts are not new to the Church. They may, however, be new to us and the very existence of a renewal to restore charisms shows that these gifts are, or have been, largely unknown to the Church at large. Charisms are spiritual gifts for service belonging to the Holy Spirit and those who manifest them are merely messengers – they are given something to deliver.

With the rediscovery of the power gifts of the Spirit during this century it is very important to keep a wise and healthy balance between the two empowerings of the Holy Spirit. '. . . You will receive power when the Spirit comes on you, and then you will be my witnesses not only in Jerusalem but throughout Judaea and Samaria, and indeed to the ends of the earth' (Acts 1:8). That power entails both the power to die to self and the power to do wonders in the service of others.

In this book, I will begin by examining the personal empowering of the Holy Spirit to make effective in us what Christ has achieved on the cross. I will then go on to look in detail at the various charisms or spiritual gifts, attempting to show what each gift means and how we might be more open to receiving them in our lives and the life of the Church. I will end by briefly examining the thorny question of baptism in the Spirit and assessing the value of prayer meetings.

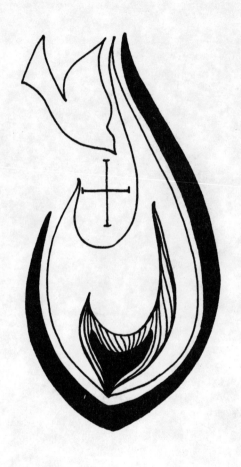

1

Holy Spirit as Guide

It is quite possible to grow up in a Christian environment and to be seen as a practising Christian attending church regularly, and yet fail to grasp the main point of the gospel. I know this is true because it happened to me.

The best teaching in the world does not guarantee that it is perfectly received. I do not actually believe that I had the best teachers possible, but that is neither here nor there, for it is what is received that matters and that may not have much to do with what is given. Much can happen to the message from the moment it leaves the teacher and the moment it arrives in the recipient.

I certainly believed that Jesus Christ was the Son of God and that he had come among us to save us; but my understanding of him as saviour was that he had come as an example to teach us how to live so that we could merit salvation. In other words everything he did or said was as an example for us. Therefore his dying was an example of how we too must obey God no matter what the cost. His rising was, for me, a confirmation that he was God and therefore we had better listen to all he had taught and obey him.

These wrong ideas of mine, and how subtle the mistake was, made it perfectly possible to listen to sermons, especially moralistic ones, and yet never have my errors challenged. The more I heard about discipline, the harder I tried to live the perfect life. I admired goodness and I was encouraged to work hard at it. Reading lives of saints was a great source of inspiration and I felt a desire to imitate them. Even when I heard about Jesus dying for me, I still saw it as a heroic example and one that inspired me to greater efforts.

This way of thinking received a shattering blow when I heard the good news of the gospel being spelt out very clearly by people of the Protestant Church. Like Luther, I suddenly realised that I did not save myself, in fact I had already been saved by all that Jesus had done at Calvary. Such a revelation was devastating and it took all my courage to allow myself to listen to my new understandings and to explore them.

I think we often imagine that once we are baptised then we are evangelised; so the tendency is for the Church to teach the baptised doctrines and church practices, which I suppose is the old idea of what catechism was about. There is, I believe, a desperate need for the baptised actually to be evangelised. To evangelise means to bring someone to understand that God so loved the world that he sent his Son to take on himself our sins and suffer the consequence in our place. Evangelisation is not something that happens once. True there is a first moment when we see what the gospel means, but then it takes all our life to accept it fully and to permit it to change us completely.

In this process of acceptance and change, the Holy Spirit acts as our guide. Jesus promised to send us his Holy Spirit telling us that the Spirit would lead us into truth, teaching us and reminding us of all that Jesus had said (John 14:26; 16:13). The Holy Spirit works directly on our spirit and we come to know the truth without really being able to say how or why we know it. It is less a matter of human reasoning than of inspiration. When we read Scripture, for example, we can understand a certain amount with our minds, but in order to have a deep knowledge in our hearts we need the guidance and inspiration of the Holy Spirit.

In my own experience I think I imagined that a flood of insights would hit me if I really gave time to reading Scripture. I had been fascinated and thrilled when I had listened to some Protestant preachers expound the Bible. They seemed to have such insights and were able to draw so much from texts that had remained a closed book to me. I think I imagined that the Spirit would enable me to see all the nuances provided I gave time to the study of the Word.

The reality was different. I did not get exciting insights and good material for sermons; what I found instead was that I began to trust what the Word said. It was not clever understandings that came, rather a conviction that this was God's Word and with it came a great desire to trust the Word and to live it no matter what. I was not advancing in understanding, but rather in knowing that God had spoken and it was my duty to obey.

This is how the Spirit works, less through human reasoning than through conviction and a deep moving in our hearts. Human intelligence is important, but in the realm of the Spirit it is limited; we certainly need to ponder and reflect but always remembering that firm assurance of faith is beyond the human intellect.

REFLECTIONS

- It is important to know how we really think of God. We may be able to give the right answers, such as he is loving, kind, merciful, but are they our answers? Or are we giving the responses we have learnt? We must not worry if our answers are wrong. The first step in putting them right is to know they are wrong.
- Try and be honest while you think about how you experience God. It may be helpful to write down what you feel.
- Then simply tell God how you feel, ask his forgiveness and ask the Spirit, who is in you, to lead you into the truth.
- As you read the next chapter compare your ideas about God with what God has said about himself through his Church and Scripture. Also see how much he has done for us.

2

The Good News

The Holy Spirit is able to convict us of the truth in Scripture, but in order to understand these truths properly we need good teaching. We cannot accept the truth and obey it until we first learn it.

I have been a priest long enough to realise that there are still many who imagine heaven and eternal life are merited by being good or by performing some heroic act. When you mention heaven you will hear people say things like: 'I wonder if I will ever make it there?' Or 'If anyone deserves to get to heaven it is old Bill, why all life long he suffered.' 'If after all this trouble I do not make it to heaven, then I shall be very upset.' I know these remarks are not to be taken seriously, but they do reflect an attitude.

Or again we can see how quickly popular devotions spread. 'Say this prayer, it is never found to fail.' 'Do the first nine Fridays and you will get to heaven.' 'Or the first five Saturdays.' 'Have a blessed candle in your house for the three days of darkness that are to come.' 'Add this prayer in between the decades of the rosary.' 'Display this holy image in your house.' Why do we have this plethora of devotions? I fear it is because the good news has not been preached clearly and people are looking for security. I am not against devotions, nor private revelations, but when more trust is put in them than in what Jesus Christ has achieved through his death and resurrection, then something has gone seriously wrong.

There are thousands of things to know about Jesus and all that he said and did, but he came for one reason and one reason alone – and that was to save the world through his death and resurrection. It would be more than tragic if we knew a lot about Jesus but somehow never came to know the real reason for his coming.

God so loved this world that he sent his Son into our human family. Jesus, who is sinless, consents to become one of our family taking to himself 'a nature like man's sinful nature' (Romans 8:3–4, Roman Breviary) and willingly bearing the consequences of that.

When Adam sinned, he rejected God and thus he experienced separation from God. I think we need to get rid of the idea of God being angry and therefore rejecting us. It is we who have rejected him, and the consequences have fallen on us. There is nothing we can do to right this problem. But God wants to put it right, so he has sent his only Son to bear in himself the consequence of our sins, because he, being God, is able to live obedient to the Father even in a human nature made in the likeness of sinful flesh.

Sin is our refusal to live for God; we were not

made for ourselves, we are creatures and are made for God. Jesus, in consenting to stand where sin has put humankind, is saying on behalf of humankind: 'You, Father, are just and right and I, as one of the human family, willingly stand separated from you because I have been made sin in your sight. I obediently embrace this consequence of humanity's sin.'

Because Jesus is God any act of his has infinite value. By taking our sins on himself and willingly accepting the terrible separation from his beloved Father, he has removed the consequences of sin. Death was unable to hold onto the Holy One of God, so at the command of the Father Jesus rose thus starting a new race filled with new life. This does not mean the whole human family has now been automatically pardonned; but it does mean pardon and new life is available *to any one who accepts this saving act of Jesus*. This is what salvation by faith means. It means putting our trust in what Jesus has done for us. However, we cannot put our trust in this truth if we have not been taught it, and there are many, as I know by experience, for whom this is by no means clear.

St Paul puts it very clearly in his letter to the Colossians (1:27). Here we are told in no uncertain terms what God's plan is. 'God's plan is this: to make known his secret to his people, this rich and glorious secret which he has kept for all his people. And the secret is this: Christ is in you, which means you will share the glory of Christ.' It could hardly be put more clearly and so to put our trust in novenas, holy medals, certain prayers and not in Christ is to disobey. It is not that these things are wrong, but they can never be a substitute for Christ's saving work.

Immediately, now, the question of the unbeliever rises up. How can those who have never heard of Jesus, or have never come to believe in him, go to heaven? I do believe God is a merciful God and I do not want to start judging those who have a different faith. God knows everyone's story and I cannot believe he will condemn those who through no fault of their own have never heard the good news. The question I am asking is, do we, the Christian believers, really believe that Jesus is our way? By getting involved with worrying about unbelievers, we can duck the question – do we ourselves really believe?

I think there still lingers among Catholics the idea that heaven is won as a reward for good work, and such an idea makes a lot of sense because logically you will not get to heaven by being bad. It is very difficult suddenly to switch from one way of under-standing to another. My reaction to first hearing that we did not merit heaven was one of anger. 'Why, that's not fair – it means we will all get there, the good and the bad. So what's the use of being good?' It is so hard for us to understand our alienation from God. We cling to the idea that we are able to put it all right, and so we fondly go on imagining that our being nice and decent is in some way going to appease God and win our forgiveness. It is very hard for a decent, law-abiding person to see their need of redemption. Was that why Jesus commended those who were spiritually poor? They at least knew their need of a saviour.

Good works will not merit our entry into heaven.

We enter heaven through accepting what Jesus has done for us by dying and rising in obedience to the Father's will. Our good works will be rewarded *in* heaven, but not *with* heaven.

REFLECTIONS

● Up until now how have you understood salvation? As a work of Christ or as something you earn? In what way do you understand Christ's passion and death? Was he giving us a heroic example of obedience or was there something more to all he did?
● Ask the Spirit to help you understand.
● Have you understood that you do not make yourself holy by doing holy things? We first need to be holy and then we can do holy things.
● Do you now see how we become holy?

3

Through Faith

Once we have heard the truth about salvation through faith in Christ, we have conscientiously to apply it to the way we live for it is not just knowing the truth that sets us free; we also have to live it. We have to live through faith.

When our basic ideas of God and Christianity are wrong, then any subsequent idea about God will be influenced by what we already think. Our way of thinking has become a habit and we need systematically to dismantle it by replacing it with the truth. St Paul calls this 'having a new mind'. The first step along this route is to admit our basic ideas of God have been wrong, or if not wrong, far too small, and to ask his forgiveness.

Spiritual truths are not learnt quickly. It is very difficult to put our trust in what God says because often we neither feel nor are convinced that it is true. I remember once doing a six-week course with a parish group during Lent. Each week I would give them a few Scripture quotes and ask them to try and practise living those truths during the week. At the end of the first week, most of them confessed they had forgotten even to read the Scripture quotes. At the end of the second week, having remembered to read the quotes, they forgot all about them in the business of the day. After the third week, having remembered the quotes, they found they seriously doubted their truth as they tried to live them during the day. It was only in the fourth and fifth week that they began to put their trust in God's Word and to ignore their feelings and the arguments that came up as they tried to live what God said.

In the last chapter we saw what Jesus has done for us by dying and rising. This act of his is enough to save the whole of humanity. However, this does not mean that we have nothing to do. All gifts need to be *both* given *and* received. Jesus has done sufficient for our salvation and if we want this to affect us then we have to receive this gift from him.

What God is saying to us is: 'I sent my Son to take your sins on himself and die in your place. Death is for sinners, and since my Son was innocent, death could not hang onto him and at my word he rose from the dead. He has done all this for you. If you want to benefit from this then it is up to you to accept what he has done by putting your trust in his sacrifice. Then your sins will be forgiven and you will be given a new life so that you can live in a new way.'

It is this act of faith that is required of a person offering themselves for baptism. At the baptism of an infant, this act of faith is made by the parents for the child. Later that child is expected to ratify this step by his or her own act of faith in what Jesus has done. When this act of faith remains lacking either by the parents, or by the child who has never ratified it personally, then although the sacrament has been valid, it has not had its full effect because it has never been fully consented to. This can easily be remedied by that individual making a simple act of faith in what Jesus has done. In this way we fan into flame our baptism.

It is this act of faith that is often missing from people's lives. Frequently faith is thought of as assenting to God's existence, believing that Jesus is the Son of God, giving intellectual agreement to doctrines and doing one's best to live a decent life. There is, however, more to faith than that. Faith is putting our trust in what Jesus has done and not in our own achievements.

This vital act of faith is not a one-for-all-time assent. True, there is a moment when we begin to believe, but belief has to be an ongoing act. If we decide to sing a song, then in order for the song to continue, we have continually to decide to sing.

If we are going to change the way we live our lives we need to begin listening to what God has already said and shape our lives accordingly. This means we have deliberately to inform ourselves about what Jesus has said and done for us, and accept his way of doing things.

The Teachings of the Church

The Church teaches many things but not every truth is of the same value. We are encouraged to go on pilgrimages, to say the rosary, to fast, to intercede for the world, to give to charity – the list is endless.

are also pious customs such as wearing blessed
ls, scapulars, venerating holy pictures – but to
t any of these things as of more value than what
God has done for us through his Son Jesus Christ is
to be in serious error. It is of paramount importance
that we know the real teachings of the Church. Salvation comes through the death and resurrection of
Jesus Christ. This does not mean we have to embark
on an academic course, but we do need to know
what God has said and done for us so as to be able
to put our trust in him.

The Importance of Scripture

Scripture remained largely closed to me until I had
learnt the good news that I do not save myself. I
then began to see that message of salvation in all
I read in Scripture, and I have become more and
more convinced that it is only after we have been
evangelised that our minds become open to receive
this message.

One of the difficulties of grasping the message of
salvation is we are told that *something has been done
but we do not yet experience it as having been done*. Scripture tells me to believe that I have been saved, but I
have to face the problem that I do not appear to be
saved by the way I live my life. The problem is it
takes time to change from trusting in what one thinks
one can do to trusting in what the Lord has done for
us. Imagine that you are having to study a certain
subject and you feel it is far beyond you; but you
have a good friend who promises to help you. That
help is always available to you, but you do not benefit from it until you go and ask for it. We are called

upon to believe that he, who conquered the evil one, is dwelling within us ready to share his power with us. We will never benefit from this power until we draw on it. To live by faith is to live in this truth.

Knowing that Jesus Christ died on the Cross for our sins is not the same as accepting this truth as something that personally affects us. It is all too easy to say, 'Lord, by your Cross and Resurrection, you have set us free' and then live as though we become free by our will-power alone.

We need to avoid two extremes: one which says 'Alleluia. Jesus has done it all, there is nothing left to do', and the other which is the attitude, 'It is all up to me.' We must remember that those who refuse to go into the sunshine will never get a suntan. This is the heart of the gospel and from it all else springs. This is the power Paul referred to when he said, 'I am not ashamed of the good news: it is the power of God saving those who believe' (Romans 1:16).

Prayer

St Benedict began his Rule with the words: 'Listen to the words of the Master'. The word 'rule' was not a help to me when I entered the monastery, because it only confirmed the idea to me that it was all up to me. I tended to look at the Rule as instruction on how to become holy. I felt that if I did everything as the Rule said, then I would achieve sanctity.

That was to misunderstand St Benedict. It was not surprising that I should do this since I had misunderstood the gospel, and this again confirms to me that we must never assume other people have been evangelised. They may appear very zealous and keen, but that could all be the result of being misled.

St Benedict was saying that if you spend time listening to Scripture, listening to the fathers, and to your superiors, then, if you have really listened (and how hard that is), you will have heard what God has done for you. Then you will begin to understand that it is not up to you to achieve but to allow God to achieve Christ's work in you.

Obviously if we are to listen to God, the fathers and our teachers, some discipline will be required on our part, but after we begin to hear God's loving plan, 'our hearts shall be enlarged, and we shall run with unspeakable sweetness of love in the way of God's commandments. . .' (Prologue: Rule of St Benedict).

Prayer is a dialogue, preferably with God speaking first. It is only by listening to God that we will begin to hear what he has already done and we will ask with fervour that his will be done.

Having listened to God, and that means having allowed God's ideas really to enter our minds and not to have gone dancing off with some idea that was our own, he now waits to hear our response. When the Church prays she puts before us what God has done and then she puts words of adoration, worship and thanksgiving into our mouths. The more we allow the Spirit of God to enlighten us with God's plans, the more we will want to express our love and thanksgiving. I am not talking about an emotion here. No matter what we may feel like God has done great things for us and he is worthy always of our thanks. Praising and blessing God is an act of faith, and as we have seen, faith saves us. So we need to spend time in prayer to God and much of that prayer will be a response in gratitude to God for what he has done.

Action

We need to do more, though, than read, study and pray. All this must bear fruit in action. As we acquire new minds so our actions ought to change. Actions that do not spring from the power of the One who dwells within us, remain just human actions and will be either laboured or cold. As we begin to allow the divine nature to possess us, then our actions become his. There is a difference between doing charitable acts and being charitable. I used to imagine that if I did kind things then I would become kind. I now realise it is the other way round, I have to be kind to do genuinely kind acts to others. If I am to be kind then I need a total transformation, something impossible for me but more than possible for God. Jesus tells us to love one another as he loves us – an impossible action unless he himself loves others through us. We are not called to imitate Christ, but to be one with him.

For this to happen we have much to do. Paul tells us to 'give up your old way of life; you must put aside your old self, which gets corrupted by following illusory desires. Your mind must be renewed by a spiritual revolution. . .' (Eph. 4:22–3). Matthew tells us that the kingdom of heaven is taken by violence (Matt. 11:12). What we must remember is that the force for this violence does not come from mere human power, it comes from the new life within. Our battle is to get our wills in line with the One who lives within us. Our self-seeking wills need to be put to death, not by our power, but by the death of Christ.

REFLECTIONS

- What is important is to try to live, not by our feelings, not by our reasoning, but by the truth. There is a power within us. We do not learn to use this power overnight. Someone once said: 'Self-will dies half an hour after we do.'
- Try taking one truth and spending some time meditating upon it. See if you are able to let that truth affect the way you live your life today. In the evening see how you did. It took time to learn to ride a bicycle. Rome was not built in a day. Steady perseverance is necessary.

4

Sacraments

As well as having a living faith which constantly brings Jesus' saving power to us, there is another way in which we receive what Christ has done for us: this way is through the sacraments.

Although God has chosen to work through sacraments, he is not obliged to do so and he is not restricted to working through them. He is God and he can give his gifts to whomsoever he wishes and in whatever way he wishes. Sacraments are for our comfort. Whenever we see certain signs and hear certain words, provided there is no obstacle on our part, then we have the guarantee of the Church that what Jesus achieved all those centuries ago is now being made effective in us. This is of great comfort because it is not a matter of feeling that something is happening, nor of understanding how it happens – it is a matter of believing and receiving.

Baptism

To begin with, obviously, baptism was given to adults who had freely chosen to be united with Jesus, and had asked to be baptised into the body of believers. Faith was required of these candidates.

With the high rate of infant mortality, parents became anxious when their children died before being old enough to receive baptism, and this prompted the Church to grant permission for infants to be baptised. The act of faith was now required from the parents and godparents, whose duty it was to lead the child to make his or her personal act of faith and acceptance when a suitable age was reached.

I have great sympathy with the Baptists who insist on adult baptism, because when parents fail to lead their children to make their own act of acceptance, we can end up with baptised people who have never appropriated their baptism. The Catholic Church accepts infant baptism and holds that such a sacrament is valid, but if that sacrament is not fully accepted at a later date, then in some way the full effect of the baptism is blocked. We must remember that sacraments are not magic, they need to be accepted deliberately.

We are born sinners; we do not become sinners by sinning, rather we sin because we are sinners. On Calvary, Jesus, who had been born into wounded nature, laid down that nature in death. In doing this he paid abundantly for all human sins. When he rose he did not come back to life in his Adam nature, he rose to new life and became the new Adam, the initiator of a new family.

Jesus told us that in order to enter this family, we had to be born of water and the Holy Spirit. We, too, have to die as he did to the Adam life, and rise to new life. We do this in Christ. What Christ did two thousand years ago is made present and active to us through the Holy Spirit.

Sacraments make real what they portray. In baptism we go down into the water signifying going into the tomb with Christ, laying down our Adam life. Rising up out of the water we rise to new life in Christ. What happened at Calvary has now happened in us. All this takes place within our spirit, we do not sense this new life in any other way. It is only as we draw on it in faith that we will experience its power. Being born of the Spirit does not give us instant spiritual maturity, just as natural birth did not give us a fully developed, mature human nature. Very slowly and gradually we acquire human skills, and this is also true in the spiritual life.

As we will see later when we talk about being baptised in the Holy Spirit, the charismatic renewal has brought many baptised adults to appropriate their infant baptism. If someone is left a fortune but never told about it, then that fortune is of no profit. And so it is with baptism: many have come to understand who they are in Christ Jesus and thus have experienced a surge of new life within themselves.

Eucharist

As we have seen, on Calvary Jesus paid for our sins, and all Christians have continually to put their trust

in what happened there. At the last supper when
Jesus commanded his disciples to 'do this in memory
of me' (Luke 22:19), I am sure they did not realise at
first just what he was asking them to do. For when
he took bread and said 'This is my body' and then
took wine and said 'This is the cup of my blood', he
was making it possible for his sacrifice on Calvary,
where his body and blood were separated, to be
made ever-present to his Church.

At Mass we do not repeat Calvary, that cannot
be done, but we make it present to us through the
sacrament, so that we may allow it to have deeper
and deeper effect in us as we bow before the mystery
made present.

God in his great mercy allows us the opportunity,
time and time again, to say our 'yes' and 'thanks' to
his Son who gave his life for us. This is wonderfully
expressed in the words of some of the prayers said
over the gifts, as the following examples illustrate.
'Father, may we celebrate the Eucharist with rever-
ence and love, for when we proclaim the death of
the Lord, you continue the work of his redemption'
(second Sunday of the year, cycle A). The same idea
is expressed in the nineteenth Sunday: 'God of
power, Giver of the gifts we bring, accept the offering
of your Church and make it the sacrament of our
salvation', and again on the twenty-seventh Sunday:
'Father, receive these gifts which our Lord Jesus
Christ has asked us to offer in his memory. May
our obedient service bring us to the fulness of your
redemption.'

Through faith and this sacrament, we are able to
expose ourselves to the mighty salvation which took
place on Calvary. Through our uniting ourselves to

Jesus by eating and drinking his body and blood we embrace and make ourselves one with the Lord who has stood in for us and paid our debt. Again what has happened in the past is made effective to us every time we celebrate the eucharist.

Reconciliation

Although Jesus empowered his disciples to forgive sins, we have no record of this sacrament until the third century. This does not mean it did not happen, only that we have no record of it.

The words of absolution, now thankfully said in English, give us a clear picture of what is taking place.

God, the Father of mercies, through the death and resurrection of his Son has reconciled the world to himself and sent the Holy Spirit among us for the forgiveness of sins; through the ministry of the Church may God give you pardon and peace, and I absolve you from your sins in the name of the Father, and of the Son, and of the Holy Spirit. Amen.

Again, a past event is now, through the work of the Holy Spirit, being applied to someone who has confessed sins. Of course it is perfectly possible and right to confess to God in the privacy of our hearts, but it is for our comfort and consolation to be able to hear the Church say with full authority, 'I absolve you from your sins.'

So, too, with the other sacraments, the saving work of the Lord is demonstrated either through healing or equipping the recipient with salvation. In confirmation the Spirit of God brings us to a deeper level of maturity as children in God, able to give and receive spiritual gifts. In marriage we need a share in the love of God in order to be faithful and loving; we need courage to face the problems of life together, the problems of family and the heartbreaks of life. When sickness strikes we need to allow the healing hand of the Lord to be laid on us through the sacrament of healing.

God in his mercy and love has arranged that we can live a life in which his Son's redeeming work is always available for us to apply to ourselves. Sacraments are received at certain moments in life, but faith is always available for us to use.

REFLECTIONS

● Many of us are familiar with sacraments. Try and note any new insights you may have received from realising that sacraments are making effective in us what was achieved long ago. For example, I used to think that if I made a good confession then God forgave me my sins at that moment. I now understand that at the moment of confession he applies the forgiveness already won for me.

● Can you see the Mass now as Calvary made present and not repeated?

● Jesus is still present to us in 'his' Church and through the sacraments we can approach him and allow him to lay his hands on us, healing us, forgiving us, strengthening us.

- In the next chapter we turn our attention to the gifts of the Spirit or charisms as they are often known.

5

Gifts of the Holy Spirit

The object of the charismatic renewal is not to establish prayer groups, rather it is to restore to the ordinary life of the Church the charisms, the spiritual gifts, the power gifts of the Holy Spirit. A charismatic gift is in operation when the Holy Spirit empowers someone to act in a way above their normal capability in service to another.

The word 'charismatic' is understood by many as denoting a lively character or an enthusiastic form of behaviour. Any person or behaviour that is exuberant, demonstrative or emotional is labelled 'charismatic'. Hence, for many 'charismatic renewal' means learning to pray with enthusiasm, with bodily gestures such as hand-clapping or raising arms into the air. I can understand how people can get this impression, but the fact is it is a wrong understanding. Such demonstrable behaviour need not be there, but if it is, perhaps it is giving expression to a deep joy.

As I say, charisms are spiritual gifts given, not for

ourselves, but in service of others. They are different from natural gifts which we use and develop for others at will; for example a teacher teaches others, a doctor through skill heals, a lorry driver transports goods from one part of the country to another. Spiritual gifts cannot be used at will. They are given at a certain moment and they should be handed on to another for their spiritual help. These gifts can bring healings through the spirit, spiritual messages or insights, miracles, or spiritual encouragement.

Spiritual gifts were certainly active in the early Church. Scripture refers to them in different books and we meet them in the early history of the Church. I think there are several reasons to explain why these gifts became almost lost to the Church. One reason has to do with the level of faith of believers. The early Church naturally attracted very dedicated people because to be a Christian in those days meant that you certainly lost your job and most likely your life. Therefore the Church's members would be people of deep faith, and where there is deep faith God can act with power. When Christianity became the religion of the Roman Empire many joined the Church for convenience, and the level of faith would have dropped markedly.

A second reason has to do with the growth of the Church. As it grew and expanded there came a need for more organisation, more legislation, more guidelines for decision making. This way of operating is in contrast to the exercise of spiritual gifts, which of their nature are inspirational. These two things, though, are not meant to be in opposition to each other, but are intended rather to be in healthy tension. If the Church becomes purely institutional, then it loses its vision and becomes just an organisation. When the Church depends on inspirational guidance alone, it can easily be misled.

However, the gifts never entirely disappeared and they would often manifest themselves in the lives of saints. Unfortunately this made people think that these gifts belonged only to the specially holy. Of course, it could be pointed out that saints are only normal Christians, and the rest of us are sub-normal. It is only in this century, however, that there has been a real rediscovery of the gifts of the Spirit and a renewed awareness that they are gifts for all Christians, not just a chosen few.

All Christians are filled with the Holy Spirit at baptism and are indwelt by him to enable us to live lives of faith and love; we have a responsibility to nurture the Spirit within us and to live by his promptings. However, the gifts of the Spirit are different. They are given specifically for the service of others and belong to the Holy Spirit, that is why we call them his gifts, and he, as it were, lends them to us for a certain moment for us to use. A prophet cannot prophesy at will. These gifts do not belong to us, and therefore we cannot turn them on as and when we desire. This is why all spiritual gifts must be tested; it is important to know which spirit acted – the Holy Spirit, the human spirit, or an evil one.

When a sacrament is given, there is no need for us to ask which spirit has operated. We have the guarantee of the Church, provided all was valid and legitimate, that God has acted; but when a spiritual gift is being used, we have no guarantee that God is the source of the gift. That is why all gifts must be tested. We will look at how they may be tested later on, but for the moment it must be understood that these gifts are not to be taken as God-given until proved.

The gifts of the Spirit must also not be confused with the fruit of the Spirit. The fruit of the Spirit is a sign of holiness, the gifts are not necessarily so. If you have a fruit tree and it produces good fruit, then you know you have a good tree. But if you have a Christmas tree loaded with the most expensive gifts, then those gifts tell you nothing about the tree.

Usually when a spiritual gift is manifested, then the person from whom it comes is used beyond their normal capabilities. Sometimes the Holy Spirit can enhance a natural gift, using the person in a way that is beyond their normal power. For example, someone with a gift for playing the guitar may be so anointed that they play the instrument in such a way as to anoint everyone who hears it at that time; or a person who is good with words may be anointed so that what they say moves people's hearts strongly.

The gifts are certainly scriptural, and in Mark's Gospel Jesus himself refers to them as signs of the believer (Mark 16:17). Some scholars claim this passage was not written by Mark but by someone else, but nevertheless it is part of the canonically accepted Gospel. St Paul refers to the charisms in his letters to the Romans, Ephesians and particularly to the Christians at Corinth. He explains these gifts in chapters 12 and 14 of his first letter to the Corinthians.

In this letter he gives a list of nine gifts of the Spirit. He starts off by saying that he wants to clear up a misunderstanding with regard to these gifts – he could well be writing today as there are certainly many misunderstandings around. There are a number of people who simply do not know about these gifts. They never seem to have heard of them, or if they have they have dismissed them as something belonging to past history. There are others who know about these gifts but simply are frightened of them and, if they are in a position to oppose them, then they do. Then there are those who misunderstand them and misuse them; as someone once said: 'I wish those who have not been given these gifts, would stop using them.' And there are those who learn about them and are open to them, but are wise and prayerful people listening to the Lord.

The nine gifts listed by Paul in his letter to the Corinthians can be divided into three sets of three. There are three which could be classed as 'doing gifts': faith, miracles and healing; there are three that could be termed 'spoken gifts': tongues, interpretation and prophecy; and there are three which could be identified as 'knowing gifts': words of knowledge, words of wisdom and discernment.

In the rest of this book, I will examine each of the gifts, and I hope we can come to understand better their purpose and the need for them to be a part of the ongoing life of the Church.

REFLECTIONS

● When did you first hear about charismatic gifts?
● Have you ever experienced others using the gifts of the Holy Spirit? Have you ever been used yourself?
● Try not to judge the gifts by whether you like

them or agree with them, but rather judge them by seeing if God gave them to his Church.

● Read what the Second Vatican Council documents say about charisms (Chapter 12 on the Church). This is the official teaching of the Church on the subject, and no matter what any priest may say to the contrary, it is still the official teaching of the Church.

● Cardinal Suenens said that if you light a candle you will give light, but you will also attract mosquitoes. The renewal certainly has attracted some odd bods, but we need to remember that everyone is loved by God and precious in his eyes.

6

Gift of Faith

'. . . Another the gift of faith given by the same Spirit'.
(1 Corinthians 12:9)

 The charismatic gift of faith must not be confused with the theological virtue of faith. The charismatic gift is a passing power by which God moves someone to act with certitude. This certitude does not come from human reasoning; it comes from the Holy Spirit and causes a person to act with confidence as when the centurian said to Jesus: 'Sir, I am not worthy to have you under my roof; just give the word and my servant will be cured' (Matthew 8:8). This charismatic gift of faith is what moves mountains and is given only at certain moments in our lives. The virtue of faith, on the other hand, is a power which Christians have all the time. It is a condition of mind, a readiness to believe the gospel.

Many of the Old Testament figures, who already believed in God, also believed God's promises given at particular moments during their lives. Noah, for example, built an ark trusting in the Lord's word that there would be a flood (Genesis 6:13ff). I am sure as he built it he came in for quite a bit of ridicule and mockery, but he carried on regardless. Abraham left his home and country on the word of the Lord to go to a land he did not know (Genesis 12:1, 2). God told Moses at the Sea of Reeds to stretch out his hand and part the waters so that the sons of Israel could pass through (Exodus 14:16). This was no easy command to obey even if Moses heard God's actual voice.

However, the Old Testament is shrouded in the mists of time and we are quite prepared to accept that things happened then that we would not countenance now. When Scripture says that the Lord told Moses, we tend to take that literally; but if someone today said to us that the Lord had told them to do this or that, we would be highly suspicious. One reason for this is that it is not our experience to hear God speak like that. Also, it sounds just too easy to have God directing us from heaven. And anyway, if a person does hear a voice, whose voice is it? I wonder if we have become so rationalistic that we have left God no room to move?

With things of the Spirit we need a very balanced attitude. It is so easy to become totally gullible and believe everything on the one hand or to become a hard-nosed cynic on the other. It is far easier to look after a graveyard than a school-yard. In the former nothing happens, in the latter there is life, tears and laughter. If the spiritual gifts are to find their place in a parish, they will cause problems; and that is why love must be pre-eminent.

I cannot say that this gift of faith has been very

prominent in my own life, though I do remember that when I was wrestling over my call to be a monk, I read a phrase in *The Imitation of Christ* which totally changed my view of my vocation. I had entered the monastery at the age of nineteen and had spent four miserable years there feeling I ought to be a monk. Finally I left and had five glorious years in the world, though I have to confess that I could not settle down to any job. After my mother died I made a retreat and the retreat-giver told me to read *The Imitation of Christ*. It was not my favourite book at that time but I decided that since he had told me to do it, I would do it. I picked up the book and the first phrase I read was: 'Why are you always seeking to rest, since you were born to labour?' I confess it is not a very exciting phrase, but from that moment on I knew I was called to be a monk, and I have never wavered since then. I know that as I read the phrase it was as though I heard the Lord speaking to me. I did not hear a voice, but I knew with utter certainty that God had spoken.

This all happened long before I encountered the charismatic renewal, and even today if I ever tell the story I can feel people distancing themselves from me. After all it sounds quite wacky.

The trouble is when someone has a strong sense that they are being called by God to do something and we need to discern whether or not this is so, we cannot rely on human prudence. Prudence is a very important virtue, but cowardice can often parade as prudence. Again if we are not endeavouring to live in the Spirit then we will find it very difficult to recognise when a spiritual gift is operating. To live in the Spirit is to live, not by our feelings, nor by our reason but by God's prompting. The problem is, what *is* God's prompting?

I have seen simple folk step out in faith to believe that God is asking something of them, only to have it proved that they were wrong. I knew a couple who had been told that a healing would take place. I certainly admired their tenacious hold on the promise while the sick person was visibly fading in front of our eyes. When the person died, the result was devastating. Yet I have seen others obey a word, and time has proved that they were correct as, for example, when a mother listening to a talk on healing, felt strongly she should ask the speaker to pray over her small son. She obeyed the prompting and the child was set free from his problem.

I can well understand why priests feel very vulnerable when they are asked to give opinions on spiritual manifestations. We feel quite inadequate, particularly in the light of the fact that we ourselves were given very poor training in this area save that we must be very, very cautious. It is no wonder that the Church is so long in making pronouncements with regard to extraordinary phenomena. It is so easy to be carried away on the one hand or be too cautious on the other. There is, in fact, the warning in Scripture of even the chosen being deceived (Matthew 24:24).

As with all spiritual gifts they must be tested. This is done by prayer, a certain amount of common sense, and endeavouring to judge what sort of person is manifesting the gift, but all the time aware that 'God's ways are not our ways'. He can ask for something that by human wisdom seems foolish (building an ark); he can use people we would not choose (Moses stuttered); he can bring about what to us seems impossible (he multiplied bread). This is where the charismatic gift of discernment is so helpful. (I will talk about this in a later chapter.) But when we do not have this gift among us we cannot force it to be there. In its place we have to use human wisdom, which is so limited.

All members of a group should be called upon to help in the process of discernment. If someone has spoken what seems like a word of faith then we need to ask if others in the group have a text from Scripture to support what was said, or another word or a prompting. How did people feel when the word was spoken? What was the gut reaction? What is important is that we be as simple as doves yet as wise as serpents.

I have to confess that I have not had too much experience with the charismatic gift of faith. I have heard about groups feeling certain they were called to do something that put them into debt, and the debt was finally met on the very last day before the deadline by an anonymous donor sending a cheque for the exact amount without knowing anything about the debt at all. But, as I say, discernment within the group is essential.

It is not always easy to draw a line between the gifts, nor to decide which gift is operating. Sometimes healers know beforehand that someone will be healed, in which case either the gift of knowledge or the gift of faith is operating. At other times they have a tingling in their hands; I do not know what gift, if any, is in operation then – the tingling happens but is not necessary. There are other times when they just lay their hands upon individuals and healings follow; we then know a gift of healing was there. The charismatic gift of faith is a call to act and not just a call to believe in a doctrine.

Teaching about all these gifts is very important and then people should be encouraged to step out in response to the slightest promptings. Absolute honesty is of utmost importance. Mistakes will be made, and correction must be given. These gifts will never be used perfectly, a lot of human nature will get mixed up in them. That is why Paul insisted that wherever these gifts operate love must be over all.

REFLECTIONS

● Have you ever been taught about this charismatic gift of faith?

● This charismatic gift must be distinguished from the virtue of faith. A Christian always has the virtue of faith; it is there to be drawn upon. For example, believing what God has accomplished through the death and resurrection of Jesus enables us to live in the power of the Risen Lord. A charismatic gift of faith is a passing gift enabling someone to act with certitude in a certain situation. Try and think of examples of faith as a virtue and faith as a charismatic gift.

● Have you ever had a strong sense that you ought to do something? Perhaps you could not give any clear reason why, except that you felt obliged to do it. Did you respond to that prompting? What happened?

7

Miracles

'. . . One may have the power of miracles'.
(1 Corinthians 12:10)

A miracle happens when God overrides or suspends the laws of nature. God is the cause of everything, and when he created this earth he gave certain natural laws so that there would be order in the universe. If and when it seems good for him to bypass those laws then, of course, being God he is free to do so. When Jesus multiplied the bread and the fishes, then the laws of nature were overridden.

There are times when it appears that the laws of nature have been suspended, but some trick may have been used to make it appear that way. A miracle is when it has been proved that there is no natural explanation for what has happened. This is why the Church is slow to accept miracles and careful and thorough investigation has first to be carried out. Coincidences are not miracles. If you have prayed for a parking spot outside the supermarket and as you drive in a car drives out, that is not a miracle for no law of nature has been suspended. If, however, the car drives out without a driver, then you have every reason to suspect that you are witnessing a miracle.

Jesus did many wonders and miracles in his lifetime for he was inaugurating the kingdom of his Father showing by his works of power who was master on earth. Adam and Eve had been given the earth and made responsible for its development. When they submitted to Satan, the earth became his. Jesus came to claim the earth back for the Father and he shows by his power that he is master of the earth.

While I was growing up I was taught that miracles and healings could still happen today, but I was also led to believe that they would be very rare and the chances of my ever seeing one of these marvels was extremely remote. If I am honest, my experience of religion was not one of liberation, for I was encouraged to embrace sufferings, carry the cross and be suspicious of anything I enjoyed. I do not think I was craving to do evil, I just seemed to want to enjoy life. Discovering that the Lord was actually on my side, made me see the gospel in a different way. There was a victorious side to it, a side that said the Lord had overcome and in him I was able also to overcome and the Church's task was to administer the fruits of his victory to the faithful.

It was easy to conclude from my experiences that the reason why we had not witnessed any signs and wonders was because we had simply never dreamt they were possible. In the early days of the charismatic renewal I remember plucking up the courage to step out in faith and pray for a healing, and while a few good things did happen, there were no major miracles. But elsewhere things were happening and even if you take into account that stories are bound to get embroidered with the telling, there was no doubt that something was stirring. They were heady times.

What I found frustrating was that I never saw any major demonstration of divine power myself. I heard about them, talked to those for whom something wonderful had happened, but I never seemed to be there when they took place. As time went by we had to face the problem that although great things were happening, these things did not always occur when we prayed for them. Clearly, although we had over the years neglected this tremendous power given to us by the Lord, this power was not something we could demand and so solve the problem of suffering and hardship.

It is important to see that there are two themes in the gospel. The first talks about surrendering, letting go, losing life, dying, offering the other cheek and denying oneself. It could be called the way of 'negativa'. The other is in sharp contrast for it talks about victory, triumph, healing, setting free, driving evil away and establishing the kingdom of God.

Both themes are in the gospel and to stress one against the other is to give an imbalance to the message. Any over-stress on the 'via negativa' will give a very distorted picture to the gospel. If the gospel of triumph is highlighted, then false expectations are raised and we can end up believing that all our problems and difficulties will be removed if only we can muster up enough faith to claim

victories left, right and centre. To adopt such thinking is to head for trouble.

Jesus experienced both these sides of the gospel.
He certainly saw power and victory in the early days
of his public life. He cast out many evil spirits, healed
many sick and calmed the storm on the sea of Gali-
lee. Yet, none of those triumphs actually conquered
Satan, they only drove him out from where he was,
leaving him free to fight elsewhere. What finally conquered him was not some mighty, spectacular contest
whereby victory came as a result of supreme power;
it all came about as the result of powerlessness.

Here we face a mystery: God's plan was not to
rout Satan by sheer force, rather he overcame him
with what seemed like a surrender – a defeat. Jesus
had the power to step off the cross, to blaze against
the powers of hell with supreme power; but the
Father's way was completely different, it was one of
humble obedience. Adam and Eve, in a world where
all was in harmony, had refused to obey God and
had gone their own way. Now here was one of their
own race submitting himself to the most difficult
obedience in a world full of sorrow and disharmony.
The holy One of God allowed himself to be stripped
of everything, his clothes, his dignity, his friends,
even his very life, and he stood in powerlessness in
obedience to his Father. It was this submission to
obedient weakness that undid the bid for indepen-
dence enacted by our first parents and all their
children. This man, who obeyed no matter what, was
God and therefore his obedience was able to
undo all the wilful acts of disobedience of his
brothers and sisters.

So when Jesus said 'Follow me', he was asking us

to follow in the way he trod, a way of victory and also apparent failure. Salvation does not just mean getting to heaven; salvation is also about being freed from ourselves. If we knew nothing but victory and success, we would never manage any humility. It is in the apparent failures where the ego can die, where we let go of what is wounded and allow ourselves to be made new.

Gifts are what they say they are – gifts. We cannot cause them to happen, but we do need to be open to their happening. There is the famous miracle of El Paso in Mexico where a parish decided that they would hold a party for the people who picked over the rubbish dumps. To their embarrassment far more people turned up for the party than they expected, but the food never ran out. We are tempted to dismiss such stories as exaggerated, even fabricated, but this has been properly authenticated. There is a video all about it and it is called *Viva Christo Rey*.

So miracles can happen today and we need to be open enough to accept that truth, yet wise enough not to jump to conclusions that any extraordinary happening is an authentic miracle.

REFLECTIONS

● Catholics usually know about miracles. They have heard about Jesus' miracles and maybe they have heard of other miracles happening at various shrines. Have you ever witnessed a miracle, heard firsthand of a miracle, or experienced a miracle in your own life?
● Do you expect ever to witness a miracle?

- Are you open to such a thing?
- Do you feel that God would never do a miracle for you?
- Do you think miracles happen today?

8

Healing

'. . . Another again the gift of healing'.
(1 Corinthians 12:9)

 In one way the healing ministry is not new to the Catholic Church for most Catholics have been brought up to believe in the healing power of God. In the New Testament we read about the many miracles that Jesus did, and, from what the Church taught and from what we read in the lives of the saints, healing has continued down through the centuries. Most of us, I am sure, have never questioned any of this for one moment, but, on the other hand, we have never expected to meet anyone who has been healed, or to experience a healing ourselves and, as for being an instrument of healing, that has probably never crossed our minds. We have been led to think of healing as something very rare and special. We tend to believe that healing is for very holy people or that it only happens at shrines.

It was only when I became involved in the charismatic renewal that I began to realise that the gift of healing was being manifested today and that all Christians could pray for healing, not just a special few. From the Gospels we learn that the Jews viewed suffering and sickness as a punishment from God (and I think some Christians are tainted with the same idea): 'Rabbi, who sinned, this man or his parents, for him to have been born blind?' (John 9:2) Jesus' reply was that neither he nor his parents had sinned.

Jesus seemed to treat sickness as something not willed by God for he spent so much of his public life curing those 'suffering from diseases and painful complaints of one kind or other, the possessed, epileptics, the paralysed' (Matthew 4:24). Some sickness he blamed on Satan: 'This woman, a daughter of Abraham whom Satan has held bound these eighteen years – was it not right to untie her bonds on the sabbath day?' (Luke 13:16) But he did not blame all sickness on Satan; for example Jesus told the cripple at the pool of Bethzatha 'not to sin any more, or something worse may happen to you' (John 5:14). It is also worth noting that Jesus left many sick at that pool unhealed.

Jesus clearly intended his disciples to heal in his name for he sent them out in pairs with the instruction to preach the gospel and to heal the sick (Matthew 10:1; Luke 10:1). When he gave his final commissioning before ascending into heaven, healing is only mentioned as part of that commission in Mark's Gospel (16:16ff). In the Acts of the Apostles we see the apostles continuing the healing ministry. Therefore we can conclude that the Church, descended from the apostles, should continue this work of healing today.

There is enough evidence of healing in the early Church to know it was practised. After the apostolic times one can trace tendencies that saw healing as a support to the proclamation of the gospel – in other words the primary purpose of healing was seen to be to confirm the gospel teaching rather than to relieve sickness.

With the Gnostic and Manichean influences, which downgraded the body, there was a lessening of the healing ministry, and thinking in the Church moved towards the Old Testament idea of sickness as a punishment sent by God. Together with the influence of the Irish monks who stressed extreme asceticism, the whole idea of seeking relief from suffering all but faded.

The questions asked by the reformers as to the value of physical sufferings really got little further than questions. No alternative was offered. The Council of Trent redefined the sacrament of extreme unction to confine it to those in danger of death and thus it remained until modern times. However, in spite of these attitudes, throughout this period healings did take place during the lives of saints. These healings did not come as a result of the sacrament of extreme unction being administered, for many of these saints were not priests. It is as though God was all the time waiting for the Church to return to a normal and healthy view of suffering and healing.

In truth suffering and pain are a vast mystery. Some pain is a warning and it tells us that something is not right. It alerts us to a problem and in that way is a blessing. Suffering can also produce character. If we always have everything our own way we could end up spoilt. Often I wonder if pain only came after the Fall. If Adam stubbed his toe on a rock, would it not have caused him pain, or would he have been so perfect that he would never have stubbed his toe? It is an interesting question but I suspect a red herring here.

In order for healing to occur, clearly some faith is required. Jesus often asked the person seeking healing if they believed. Who of us has enough faith? It is equally wrong to try and work up a faith. Rather, the right attitude is 'Lord, I believe, help my unbelief'. But belief does not guarantee healing. I know of a sad case where a wife got cancer, and both she and the husband desperately stated they believed that the Lord would heal her. The cancer took its course and she died. No one could say they did not have hope that the Lord would heal. But what a devastation her death was for the husband.

I do believe that God can overcome suffering without removing it. He himself had to go through death and yet look what came out of his death. I believe the Lord is often saying, 'I will walk with you through this and we will make, what is negative, into something positive.' I have sometimes met with those who say that they are resigned to God's will, and I am not sure that is right. I believe there has to be some fight in us against the sickness even while we accept that we are sick. I have heard doctors say that when there is no fight in the patient for life, then there is very little that they can do. Much depends on how we are looking at life. If we look at things from an earthly point of view, we are bound to see problems, misfortunes, sickness as obstacles which need to be removed. If we are believers then no doubt we will ask God to do this. If he does not do what we want we may feel hurt, unloved and even bitter. 'If God loves me, then how can he not listen to my prayer?'

If, however, we look at life from God's point of view of eternity, then we will see all these difficulties in a different light. They will remain difficulties and we can certainly ask God to deal with them; but we will have a trust that God who has our eternal destiny at heart, will only allow troubles which can be used for eternal profit to touch our lives. He says to us at such moments: 'You and I can make use of these disadvantages, we can turn the tables on Satan who thinks he is going to upset you, for the very plan he uses to hurt you, we, together, can use for good purposes.'

It is not God who sends the problems; we live in a world where there are problems. He permits a difficult situation, even a tragedy, promising that a deeper good can come from it. This is all but impossible to see if we are looking at life from an earth-bound perspective, where everything is judged from our own point of view.

Sickness is not confined to the body alone, it can affect the psyche or the spirit. All these areas are closely related and what is a spiritual problem can manifest itself in the body. A simple example is that having to relate to a very difficult person, can cause a tightening up of muscles whenever that person approaches. This tightening of the muscles could begin to cause the body to react in some way.

We must also be aware of 'healing spirits' invoked by certain people who claim to have a healing gift. Evil spirits can affect apparent healings. We must only seek for healing in the name of Jesus. Also there is such a thing as a natural gift of healing. No spirit is invoked but in some way healing is transmitted from one body to another. There are machines which can make the aurora around the body visible and it has been noticed that after the laying on of hands the aurora is lessened. Something has been passed from one person to the other. This form of healing seems to be more natural than spiritual.

Those who feel that God has given them a healing gift will only find confirmation by using it and seeing if results follow. Love must be the moving power in us. We must be cautious not to act insensitively, nor to force people to have us pray over them. It can be helpful to have several people praying over the same person, for if a healing does take place, then no one is able to claim it was through them that the gift came. Also, when there are several people involved, then other gifts such as words of knowledge might well be given to help to direct the focus of the prayer.

Personal Experience

It might be helpful at this point to say something about my own first attempts at praying for healing. I have to say they were not very encouraging. A parent of one of the students in the school where I taught had been diagnosed as having cancer. Immediately the thought came into my mind, 'you must go and pray for healing'. I went hot and cold at the idea of it, and this wretched thought gave me untold trouble. I went from feeling guilty and cowardly, to wanting to rush in as maybe a miracle would follow. Finally I plucked up courage and I went to visit the sick person. At the end of the visit, just before I left, I asked if I could say a short prayer. Of course this was welcomed, priests are often expected to give a blessing. I do not think I could call the prayer that I made a bold prayer for healing, I simply did not have the courage. Eventually the person concerned died of the disease and I felt badly for a long time.

Early in the 1970s I returned to England from the USA and, because I had had some experience with the renewal, I was considered rather an expert and I was asked to address a gathering in Harrogate at the Holy Child Convent. What I spoke about was the power of the gospel for today, and obviously I referred to its healing power. I gave quite a good argument that the Church should be healing today, for I had done a lot of thinking and praying since those early days in St Louis. I knew that Scripture supported this view; I had heard of enough genuine cases to be convinced myself.

I must have given a good argument for at the end of the talk, to my horror, I saw a nun hobbling up to me and I knew what she wanted. I looked around to see who else would do the praying over her, but it seemed that they had seen her coming and had fled. What else could I do, but pray over her. I made a rather safe prayer, punctuating it with such phrases as 'if it be your will'. I told the sister that it did not appear to be God's will as she did not seem any better; and she, bless her, hobbled away from me.

You do not need much imagination to guess how I felt. I drove back home to Warrington alone that night and I had plenty to say to the Lord as I drove. I complained that he had been badgering me about this healing gift, and that day I had dared to preach on it, and even dared to lay my hands on someone and pray, but where was he? Was it his half-day? I have to say here that I feel it is right to be fairly familiar with God. That particular evening I felt badly let down and so was a bit flippant with him. I got no answer during the car journey.

About three weeks later I got a phone call from Harrogate, I cannot even remember what the call was about, but at the end of it the person said, 'Oh, that nun you prayed over was not cured, but she was so much better that she went back to teaching.' My reaction was: 'What will happen when I believe?' And that, I now see, is precisely the danger with these experiences. Having been very closed to the possibility of healing we now all move to the opposite extreme and expect it to happen every time we pray.

There is no doubt that some people do have a gift for healing. This does not mean that every time they pray someone gets healed, but it has to be noted that a good number do seem to get some blessing. I do believe that all prayer is answered, but it need not necessarily be answered in the way we would wish.

I remember hearing Kathryn Kuhlman, a powerful healer belonging to a Protestant Church, and certainly things happened at her meetings. May God forgive me but I was very suspicious all the way through her sessions. First of all I found it theatrical, I did not expect to see her on the stage dressed in an evening gown. The music was sentimental and I felt uncomfortable until she started to pray. I cannot really recall, now, what she said, but I know I sensed a presence came upon us. Then she started pointing

to a certain part of the theatre saying there was someone there with arthritis and would they come down
to be prayed for. Then she would point to another
part and again say what complaint that person had
and would they come down. You were not allowed
to go on to the stage unless she had invited you. I
had been hoping to be called up there but I had no
physical complaints.

After she had gathered quite a number of people
on the stage, she began praying over them. There
was a nun who said she had not been able to touch
her toes for a time, and there she was all but doing
acrobatics, she seemed so free. Some people she did
not have to pray over, for on their way to the stage
they received their healing.

In truth I now have no trouble in praying for
healing. I do not think I have a definite gift of healing, but certainly there have been times when God
did seem to do something. There is a lady in
Cornwall who swears that after I had prayed for her
she regained the ability to sleep. There was another
lady who complained of a migraine headache and
said it had gone after I had prayed, but there was
no proving this. But the one I have never forgotten
happened when I was giving a parish mission in
Bradford. The priest said to me one evening, 'Let's
go over and see Kath, a friend of mine, who has had
an accident on a sledge and damaged her spine'. We
went over and the poor lady was certainly in much
pain. We had coffee and then my friend and I prayed
over her and went off home.

Next morning while I was preaching Kath walked
into the church. My priest friend noticed she was
walking without a limp; I was so busy preaching I

did not spot it. Needless to say there was quite a commotion afterwards when the story got out. She had not felt anything during the time we prayed over her, but she slept that night for the first time since the accident. When she got up in the morning all pain was gone. Since then she has been back to the doctor and he says she should still be in great pain, for the back is not healed. It is now eight years since this happened and she is still fine. In fact she has gone on several hill-walking holidays.

Practicalities

People need to be encouraged to pray for the sick. Praying for the sick does not mean you are going to heal the sick; you are *praying* for the sick. You are asking God to heal. Perhaps later on you may become more bold as you pray and study the Lord's commands for he did tell us that what we bind or loose on earth is bound or loosed in heaven. I know Catholics apply this text to confession only, but there are many other texts where the Lord tells us that he has put power in our hands and we are to act in his name (Luke 10:19). To keep asking him to act when he has told us to act, can be a real failure to obey his commands.

Some people have had a tingling sensation or feel great heat in their hands – these can be signs that God is trying to stir us to act. We will only know by stepping out.

So to sum up: today there is a new move to understand the Lord's command to his Church to heal. There seem to be two ways healing can be given. There is the sacrament for the sick, once known as

Extreme Unction and reserved for the dying, now called the Sacrament of the Sick, and which is given for recovery. The other is the gift of healing which can come through any member of the Christian family.

When a gift has been lying dormant for many years it needs time before it finds its right place in the normal life of the Church. Mistakes have been made, people have thought healing can be obtained on demand. We still have to grapple with the question of healing and the mystery of suffering. There is still much to understand, and doctors, psychiatrists and priests can learn much from each other.

REFLECTIONS

- Do you believe in healing today?
- Have you ever asked for healing?
- Have you ever experienced either physical or psychological or spiritual healing?
- Does the idea of healing frighten you?
- Were you taught to embrace suffering and sickness because it was God's will? If so, how do you reconcile the fact that Jesus healed so many?

9

Tongues and Interpretation

'. . . Another the gift of tongues and another the ability
to interpret them'.

(1 Corinthians 12:10)

I never paid much attention to the gift of tongues because I never felt it could be of any relevance to my life. The way I understood Pentecost was like this: the apostles, after receiving the Spirit, rushed out excitedly speaking their own language, as I thought, and were heard speaking the language of the country from where the listeners came. Not being a reader of Scripture I never, of course, came across the text in 1 Corinthians where Paul says: 'Anybody with the gift of tongues speaks to God, but not to other people; because nobody understands him when he talks in the spirit about mysterious things' (14:2). At Pentecost, as I understand it now, two miracles were happening: firstly the apostles were talking in tongues, that is a language unknown to anyone save God; secondly the bystanders heard them speaking in their own languages.

The rediscovery of this particular gift today has caused the greatest difficulty. When I first heard about tongues being used, I was suspicious but also curious. I had thought that 'speaking in tongues', whatever that meant, was what happened at the first Pentecost, but was not something people did today. What bothered me was the thought of being able to make noises as though I was speaking in a foreign language, because as a child I used to do this with my brothers. I never dreamt that I would be able to speak in tongues because I felt I would never be sure if it was me or the Holy Spirit speaking.

I came across the gift rather dramatically when I was living in the USA and was visiting a Benedictine monastery at Pecos in New Mexico. Through over-work, I think I had exhausted myself for I was feeling drained of energy and enthusiasm. At one of their prayer meetings I heard a monk praying in tongues, so I decided to do what I had learnt as a child. I said a prayer to God expressing that if he wanted me to do this, 'Well, here goes. . .' What was there to lose for I was among strangers and in a few days I would be over the hills and far away? Nothing dramatic happened – I felt rather foolish and went to bed believing there was nothing in it.

But the next day texts in Scripture and things said by the retreat-giver struck me very forcibly. It was as though I was being urged to ask myself if I really believed in the gospel. After what had been quite a long dark period for me, I seemed now to be getting some light. The question I asked myself was, 'Had this all happened because I had experimented with tongues last night?' I just do not know. Throughout that day I allowed myself to sing in tongues and I felt more and more at peace.

Not long after this I went to stay with a group of priests in Michigan who were trying to look honestly at this renewal. I was feeling fairly lost spiritually but was determined to throw myself into everything whole-heartedly. I was advised to use the gift of tongues in my own private prayer-time.

Three days later, just after I had finished doing this, I felt I suddenly understood the gospel for the first time. It was as though I heard God say: 'Why are you so afraid of me? Can't you see I have made you my son, why not live as my son?' It is strange that a truth I must have heard many, many times, suddenly burst on me as though I had heard it for the first time.

This did not mean that from then on all was plain sailing; no, I had now painfully to apply this truth to all my false attitudes, false assumptions, anxieties and fears. Slowly I began to see that the gospel was not about performance and doing one's best, but about receiving life, forgiveness and love.

It is important to remember that God deals with each of us as individuals and that my story is *my* story. I do not think everyone has to speak in tongues, though I believe it should be more common than it is; nor do I believe that everyone can learn to speak in tongues by being told to babble. It is a gift from God and for each one of us it will be different, and while some of us may need a kick-start to get us going, others will find it happens very easily.

So what is speaking in tongues all about? Basically, when people pray in tongues they allow the Holy

Spirit to pray in them using their voice to utter syllables which mean nothing to them or to anyone who might hear them, for they are directed to God. St Paul refers to this when he says: 'The Spirit too comes to help us in our weakness. For when we cannot choose words in order to pray properly, the Spirit himself expresses our plea in a way that could not be put into words. . .' (Romans 8:26).

In the description of Pentecost in the Acts of the Apostles, it is not too easy to see exactly what happened. It would seem that when the Holy Spirit came 'They were all filled with the Holy Spirit and began to speak foreign languages as the Spirit gave them the gift of speech' (Acts 2:4). Other translations say 'foreign tongues'. Does this mean the apostles spoke in a known language or did they speak in a heavenly language? It is not clear. I take this to mean that the apostles received the gift of tongues at that time. Presumably this all took place in the upper room. Then in verse 5 it goes on to talk about devout men living in Jerusalem who assembled because in some way they were attracted by the commotion. Whether these men went into the upper room, or the apostles burst out of it into the streets is not clear, but on hearing the apostles speaking they each heard them in their own tongue. So not only was the gift of tongues being manifested but also there was the miracle of everyone hearing in their own language.

Normally, however, this gift of tongues is not the ability to speak a known language that you have not learnt, though, as at Pentecost, there have been instances where someone has spoken out making noises that were unintelligible to them but which were actually a language known by someone else present. This is not really what speaking in tongues is about. Remember the text quoted earlier: 'Anybody with the gift of tongues speaks to God, but not to other people; because nobody understands him when he speaks in the spirit about mysterious things' (1 Corinthians 14:2).

This gift is mentioned a number of times in the Scriptures and Mark tells us that Jesus said it was a sign of a believer (Mark 16:17). The place where we meet it most frequently is in the Acts of the Apostles, where we see the new Church being established.

So clearly this gift was active in the early Church. St Augustine refers to it as 'singing in jubilation' in his treatise on Psalm 32 (sermon 1, 7–8). 'It means to realize that words are not enough to express what we are singing in our hearts.' I do not think that this means the gift is only used when we feel very joyful, for it can happen when we are unable to pray because of some heaviness, 'the Spirit comes to help us in our weakness' (Romans 8:26).

I think the very fact that we cannot get our reason wrapped round it, is why this gift causes so much trouble today, it makes us afraid. Whenever there is something that the human mind is not able to explain, we can become over-cautious and suspicious.

Strangely enough contemplation does not seem to have the same effect and yet that certainly is beyond the grasp of the mind. Maybe some think of contemplation as having heavenly thoughts, visions, or experiences of being taken up to the seventh heaven. In my understanding contemplation is when our mind, having thought every thought about God, decides that there is no thought that can catch

God, and so it gives up thinking and becomes more content with just knowing God is there. Not being able to find any adequate thought we are content with just loving him and being loved by him. One no longer tries to think thoughts but is content with a presence. I think in essence tongues is similar: in contemplation you cannot find suitable thoughts, in tongues you cannot find suitable words.

Our voice, of course, is very personal to us; it is unique. If anyone could use my voice they would, in a sense, possess me. They could say with my voice, 'I, Ian, say this to you'. To allow the Holy Spirit to use our voice is to surrender very deeply to him. When we pray in tongues we submit our mind, the thing we value most. Often it is the beginning of a new relationship with God, because it involves such a deep surrender. But the Holy Spirit does not force us, we have to allow it to happen.

Normally this is a private gift to be used alone, but it can and does happen that a group all feel moved at the same time to worship God in tongues. A group can sing in tongues and it is an extraordinary experience to hear a very large crowd all singing different tunes, with different sounds and yet the whole making an exceedingly beautiful harmony. I do not know of any instance in Scripture where it is reported that a group has sung in tongues. As I said earlier, St Augustine referred to singing in jubilation.

The first time I heard a group singing in tongues I was amazed at the beauty and harmony of the sound. Another strange thing was that it started quite unexpectedly and ceased just as suddenly as though some unseen conductor had given the sign. Others have found the experience quite unnerving.

In the early days of renewal when people questioned me on tongues, some asked if I would give a demonstration. I would always answer that while I could babble, I would not be sure that it was the Holy Spirit prompting me. All the gifts can be mimicked but we cannot turn genuine gifts on at will. Tongues can very easily be forced and groups need to be on their guard against feeling pressurised to use tongues when the Spirit is not prompting. I am sure most of these gifts come when we have our focus on God and not on what is going on around us. I think there has to be some prompting from within to which we respond, and as I have said, it is usually a gift to be used in private.

Tongues and their Interpretation

Not all tongues need interpreting. For clarity's sake let's call the tongue that occurs during a prayertime 'praying in tongues' and the tongue that needs interpreting 'speaking in tongues' or 'a message in tongues'.

A message in tongues is when an individual speaks out alone, loud and clear, in tongues. Everyone then should become quiet and listen. When the message finishes, all should pray that an interpretation will be given to someone. This is not a translation for no known language has been used; an interpretation is when someone senses what God wants said at that moment.

Sometimes one of the group may have been getting a thought, a prophecy, and have been wondering whether to share it or not. Tongues, coming from another, can encourage that person to speak out.

I have been present in situations when someone spoke out in tongues and we all waited for the interpretation. I wondered why the Lord did not give a prophecy in our own language; why did he have to prompt one individual to speak in tongues, and another with an interpretation? The answer could be that in this way he is showing us the unity we have in sharing the same Holy Spirit.

I was once at a small meeting when someone spoke out loud in tongues. I remember feeling tense because there were so few of us; in a large crowd you can always hope that someone will speak up. As the tongue was being spoken I had a text from Scripture in my head, but I was very new to all this so I sat there not saying a word. After what seemed an awkward time, someone spoke out the very text that was in my head. Was that a coincidence or was it God? A sceptic will say 'coincidence', a simple soul will say 'it was God'. I think a wise person will ponder deeply.

I think we all need to ponder deeply about this gift. It is in Scripture (1 Cor. 14:27–8). It is called a gift of God and we need to be careful before we reject it. God does not do anything without good reasons. The Second Vatican Council affirmed that the charisms are not just for the early Church but are for the Church of today. God's ways are not our ways.

REFLECTIONS

- Have you ever given much thought to the gift of tongues? Most people associate it with what happened at Pentecost and never dream that the gift is available to any believer. Has that happened in your case?
- Does the idea of this gift frighten you? If so why?
- Have you ever heard anyone speak in tongues?
- Have you ever, when alone, sung in a made-up language?
- Do you think God might have been prompting you to launch out into something you cannot exactly explain so as to set you free from being strictly logical?

10

Prophecy

'. . . To another the gift of prophecy'.
(1 Corinthians 12:10)

Prophecy is not about foretelling the future. Prophecy is when God reveals his heart and mind, through a person, to an individual or to a group. The message may concern the future or it may not; it could be a warning or a correction about some past event or it could be a message of comfort in a time of trial.

God spoke to his chosen people through his prophets. Moses led them out into the desert telling them that God was leading them into the promised land. Nathan was used by God to rebuke David for his sin; Isaiah spoke many messages of comfort and consolation to the Jews in exile. Prophets did not belong only to the Old Testament times. In his letter to the Ephesians, for example, Paul lists prophets among those chosen by the Lord to serve his Church (4:11).

God speaks to each of us in many ways but we often do not recognise it is God speaking. Samuel, for instance, thought it was the high priest calling him when God first spoke to him. If we are closed to the idea that God can and does speak to us, it is not likely that we will ever be used as a prophet. On the other hand if we are one of those people who is not able to tell the difference between a good idea and a God idea, then, alas, we will imagine we are getting messages when we are not. It is not easy to explain how a person knows when God has spoken to them. This is why all gifts of the Spirit need testing to see from what spirit they come. St Paul says, 'Never try to suppress the Spirit or treat the gift of prophecy with contempt; think before you do anything – hold on to what is good and avoid every form of evil' (1 Thessalonians 5:19–20). St John repeats the warning: 'It is not every spirit, my dear people, that you can trust; test them, to see if they come from God; there are many false prophets, now, in the world' (1 John 4:1). We must know which spirit is at work, God's Spirit, a human spirit or an evil one.

Obviously anything said that contradicts Scripture cannot be of God. But just because it does not contradict Scripture is no guarantee that a prophecy comes from God. Today we are witnessing a plethora of visions and locutions telling us to repent, fast, and pray. All these are good things, but it is no guarantee that it is God who is actually sending the messages. The Church adopts a long slow process before she accepts such things; we have to be as wise as serpents and as simple as doves, which is no easy task! It is far easier to be a sceptic or a naive person.

Just as in ordinary human communication, where

there can be a problem of misunderstanding or of colouring what we have heard with our own ideas, so, too, this can happen with visionaries. The vision may be of heavenly substance, but the one who receives it is still human and can err, and the message they pass on may be greatly influenced by their whole cultural background. In prophecy the message may only be 20 per cent of God and 80 per cent of the prophet. Such happenings are not done deliberately by the person giving the message, and often it takes quite a time before they become a reliable prophet giving us God's mind.

The testing that I have been talking about is very much a human gift. We deliberately test the message given by reason, by checking with Scripture and by a lot of common sense. There is also a spiritual gift of discernment, and we will talk about that in a separate chapter.

The first time I heard a prophecy given was at a prayer meeting held at the Visitation Convent in St Louis, USA. Prayer meetings were something quite new to me and I did not feel very comfortable being there. I sat right at the back so that I could make a quick get-away if something untoward happened. I was sitting on the edge of my chair feeling very awkward when suddenly in one of the quiet periods a voice spoke out very clearly: 'Why are you so afraid? Can't you see I am present?' That word went right into my heart and I was certain it was spoken to me. The person who uttered it was a long way from me and clearly they had not spoken because they saw me looking awkward. I remember thinking and asking myself, 'Why am I so afraid? I am a Benedictine and my life is spent in praising God and that is all that is happening here. True the songs are somewhat different to what I am used to, but all the same, God is being praised.'

A message spoken out during a meeting may not be relevant to everyone, and because it may not speak directly to us we must not therefore imagine it is a non-prophecy. It may well be for someone else. That is why it is a good practice for a person touched by what is said, to speak out about what the word meant to them. In a prayer group setting it is an encouragement to the person who spoke the message, and it also helps the leaders to know that the message seemed genuine. In other words it is a way of testing the message. If, on the other hand, no one responds to the prophecy, and the person who gave it is one who speaks out a lot, then the leaders of the prayer meeting may have to talk to that person so that everything may be done in peace.

It is not easy helping people know if they are being prompted by God or just a good idea. I think we need to encourage people to speak out when they feel a prompting, as it is only by trial and error that we can learn. If during a meeting a person gets a phrase or an idea, then they should be encouraged to ignore it to start with. If it keeps recurring, or if a reading from Scripture shared by another seems to confirm it, or the same happens with another spontaneous prayer or prophecy, then it is best humbly to share the thought and see if it is helpful to another. Mistakes will be made, but in love we dare with each other and we grow. Pride is in all of us and we can often be driven by a hidden desire to be of importance. As we shall see in the chapter on prayer meetings it is love, not gifts, that make prayer meetings blessed.

Prophecy is not, however, confined to the prayer meeting. During a counselling session the counsellor may be given a word for the person counselled. It could also happen in a sermon, or even when two people share spiritual thoughts together during an ordinary conversation. I heard of a priest once who during his sermon lost the thread of his thought and for a few moments while he tried to remember his plan, he just spoke out a few ideas. Afterwards in the sacristy someone came and thanked him for his sermon. Being human he was interested to know what part had been so helpful – it was the bit where he lost his theme and just filled the gap with a few words.

Writers can be prophetic and can be used powerfully by God to convey God's thinking to us. A person need not know that they are being used prophetically while they speak. It is often very difficult to distinguish between a fine thought, obviously prompted by God, and a prophecy, when God uses another in a way far above their capability. Spiritual gifts can be mixed with natural gifts; a person with a fine voice, for example, can be so anointed during a song that they lead listeners to a profound worship of God.

As with all these gifts we need to be as wise as serpents and as simple as doves. We need each other to protect ourselves from imagining that we are God's gifts to the Church. Of course, we are God's gifts to each other but not because of what we do but rather because of who we are.

REFLECTIONS

- Do you ever, while in prayer or in study of Scripture, have a sudden clear sense of understanding God's plan or purpose? It could be God is giving you insight into his mind. Jesus did promise that the Holy Spirit would lead us into truth (John 16:13). If that insight concerns another person or a situation, then it could be a prophecy.
- Have you ever while praying for someone had a clarity of God's plan for them or a sense of their inner burden? This could be a word of knowledge or a word of wisdom. Prophecy is usually a word from God to the person.

WORDS OF
WISDOM AND ✝
KNOWLEDGE

11

Words of Wisdom and Knowledge

'To one there is given through the Spirit the message
of wisdom, to another the message of knowledge by
means of the same Spirit'.

(1 Corinthians 12:8 NIV)

There are several ways of gaining knowledge. The first, the normal way, is through the use of reason. Spiritual truths, however, though not contrary to reason, are beyond it, and we need God to assist us to accept them. The Holy Spirit has to help us as we think about revealed truths. As we ponder and wrestle with them, the Holy Spirit gives us understanding that could not be reached by reason alone.

Human reason can grasp the facts of divine revelation, but we need the Spirit to give us that interior illumination that only he can give. For example, the mystery of the incarnation means that the second person of the Trinity became a human being. A person may be able to grasp the fact of the incarnation, but his reason may want to reject it because it cannot see how God, who is everywhere, can now only be somewhere; or how he who is almighty, now has limited strength. It is the Holy Spirit who is able to make such truths, which seem contrary to reason, become acceptable and life-giving.

This spiritual knowledge given by the Holy Spirit is both for our own spiritual growth and also for others. At baptism the Holy Spirit gives us gifts for our own spiritual life. At confirmation he turns us towards others so that we may become full functioning parts of the body, both receiving life and giving life. The seven gifts of confirmation are both for our own growth and also for service to others. The kind of knowledge and wisdom referred to in these gifts is the knowledge and wisdom into which the Holy Spirit leads us, as we wrestle to understand divine revelation.

In Section 11 of the documents on the Church from the Second Vatican Council we read:

Incorporated into the Church through baptism, the faithful are consecrated by their baptismal character to the exercise of the cult of the Christian religion. Reborn as sons of God, they must confess before men the faith which they have received from God through the Church. Bound more intimately to the Church through the sacrament of confirmation, they are endowed by the Holy Spirit with special strength. Hence they are more strictly obliged to spread and defend the faith by word and by deed as true witnesses of Christ.

In addition to the above there are other kinds of knowledge and wisdom, given by the Holy Spirit, which differ from what I have just described. These concern the charismatic gifts of wisdom and knowledge. With these gifts it is as though knowledge comes directly into our mind which is not the fruit of our reasoning processes or of our wrestling with revelation, but is suddenly placed there. This process is not easy to explain since it does not occur by the ordinary means of one thought leading to another, but as a direct revelation from God. If what is known is a piece of wisdom which helps to solve a difficult problem, then it is known as a word of wisdom, or a message of wisdom, or an utterance expressing wisdom. If the message concerns a known fact about something or someone, then the message is called a word of knowledge, or a message, or an utterance expressing knowledge.

When Jesus healed a man who was both dumb and blind (Matt. 12) the Pharisees, among themselves, began to accuse Jesus of casting out devils by the power of Beelzebul. We read in verse 25 that Jesus addressed the issue, 'knowing what was in their minds. . .'. One wonders whether he just guessed, or whether it was obvious from the way they were behaving, or did he have a word of knowledge? Jesus also promised his disciples that when they were brought before rulers they would be given what to say (Matt. 10:19). Clearly God can and does put words of truth directly into our minds.

Words of knowledge or wisdom usually come during a time of prayer, especially when we are praying for individuals. The way they come varies; sometimes they come as a thought into our mind or as a picture, and they usually seem to come out of the blue. Sometimes just one word comes. For example, for no apparent reason, the word 'father' could come into someone's mind, or the word 'insecure' or 'deceived', when prayers are being said over an individual. It is wise not to act immediately, but rather to leave that word in the mind and see if anything else is said that might confirm it. If it keeps returning then it is best to share it.

Some people get pictures and they can be quite vivid. I had one once which really was quite strange, but because it made no sense to me I kept quiet about it. The picture I saw in my mind's eye was of a number of people standing in a room with lampshades on their heads. The lampshades were opaque and therefore the light did not shine through them but fell on the floor. Everyone stood there in a pool of light. As I have said, because it made no sense to me I did not mention it to anybody.

Quite sometime later I remembered the picture and had an insight into its meaning. With regards to the gifts of the Spirit I had felt a little left out. I never got pictures or words of knowledge or great insights into Scripture and I complained to the Lord about it. I now felt he was teaching me something through this odd picture of people with lampshades on their heads. He seemed to be saying that if those people with the shades on their heads would only step forward one pace then the light would go with them and they would see the next step. I felt God was saying to me, 'My word gives you enough light to take the next step'.

Quite soon after that, I was praying the office when a phrase from Psalm 119 leapt out at me. It says, 'My word is a lamp for your steps' – this made me understand that the Word of God was not just to delight my mind, but was to direct my steps. I suppose that was a word of wisdom for myself. This could easily seem a bit trite but because of this experience of mine I can now understand other people's stories.

The problem with spiritual gifts that concern the mind is that they can be imagined, even contrived. Imaginative people can think a stray idea is a message from God and then we can get into all sorts of problems and trouble. That is why all gifts *must* be tested. We have to ask: was that God speaking, or was it the human spirit?

As with the other gifts, the gifts of wisdom and discernment are tested by making sure they are not contrary to Scripture or the teachings of the Church; did they hit the spot? was the word spoken true, helpful, encouraging? Obviously immature people can play havoc here, and that is why we need mature and spiritual leaders to guide and oversee what happens. Being open to the spiritual world does not necessarily mean you are in touch with God. There are good spirits and evil spirits. Jesus told us that he was the door, the gate, and that we have to come in and out through him.

Leaders need to encourage their members to use gifts. Teaching is necessary, followed by the encouragement to step out and offer their insights, their thoughts or pictures. Gradually the true gifts will be discovered. In chapter 14 of Paul's first letter to the Corinthians he shows that love is of primary importance, but he also urges the value of spiritual gifts. Gifts without love can be very divisive. Let's face it, in all of us there is ambition, a desire to be wanted, of use, valued. Love must both encourage and correct.

Teaching will help people recognise how these gifts work, and they must then be encouraged to step out and share their pictures, words, phrases. However, if these are not saying anything to anyone, then, maybe, at that moment the gift has not been given. It is important to realise that we are trying to be one body and not just a group of individuals with gifts. When one has a gift the whole body rejoices.

REFLECTIONS

- Had you ever heard about these gifts before reading this chapter?
- Do these gifts appear very strange and foreign to you?
- Even though they are scriptural, do you feel that neither of these gifts could ever be yours?
- If so why?
- Some people desire to have these gifts, some are afraid of them. Which are you?
- Can you see the value of these gifts?
- Can you also see their danger if not tested?

DISCERNMENT

12

Discernment

'. . . Another may have the gift of recognising spirits'.
(1 Corinthians 12:10)

We cannot always depend on charismatic gifts happening. They are a gift from God; we cannot make them occur. God has given us his Holy Spirit, his Church and an intelligence, and we have a responsibility to make use of these gifts; but God, when he decides, can intervene and make some charismatic gift operate to help us. We need to be open to this possibility.

I have stressed, in talking about some of the other gifts, the need for discerning what spirit is operating. This is done by testing the spirit and to do this we use human discernment, that simply means we use common sense, we check that Scripture has not been contradicted (remembering that the absence of contradiction does not guarantee genuineness), and we also find out if the message meant anything to

107

anyone – was it a strong message or just nice? We need also to consider the person who gave the message – are they stable, reliable, or perhaps highly imaginative (remembering, however, that God spoke through Shimei to David as he was being cursed by him, and also through Balaam's donkey)?

On the other hand the charismatic gift of discernment is when someone recognises which spirit is at work without having to go through the normal process of human discernment. The person just knows. This does not mean that others present should not use human discernment. They should note the fact that someone has claimed to have the gift of discernment, and then weigh that gift.

There are examples in Scripture of this gift of discernment in operation. Peter, for instance, when he confessed that Jesus was the Christ, was commended by Jesus for allowing the Father, and not flesh and blood, to reveal that truth to him (Matthew 16:17). Again, Peter discerned which spirit was working in Ananias and his wife Sapphira in the Acts of the Apostles. The converts were bringing gifts to the new community, some of them selling their properties and giving the proceeds to the apostles to help them in their work. Ananias and his wife Sapphira had sold their property, but at the suggestion of Sapphira, they kept back part of the money and presented the rest to the apostles. Peter immediately recognised that a fraud was taking place and he spoke out, accusing them of keeping back part of their gift. Clearly he assessed the situation by a gift of insight given him directly by God (Acts 5).

In the Old Testament the Psalms are full of references to God probing our hearts, knowing our thoughts, showing that God has access to our minds. 'Before ever a word is on my tongue you know it, O Lord, through and through' (Psalm 139:4). In the book of Jeremiah we read, 'I, the Lord, search to the heart, I probe the loins' (17:10). Solomon begged God: 'Give your servant a heart to understand how to discern between good and evil' (1 Kings 3:9). Evidently the people of the Old Testament comprehended that God was God and that he knew their inmost thoughts and could give inspiration directly into their hearts.

We are all subject to ideas popping into our heads and it is not easy to know exactly from where they come. They can originate from some deep-seated drive, a desire to be recognised or from a highly imaginative mind. God has access to our minds for he is our God and in his love and care he can prompt us with his inspirations.

Evil spirits also can influence us by putting false ideas into our heads in the hope that we will be led astray. So any thought that suddenly comes into our mind must always be discerned – where did that come from?

God can communicate with us in all sorts of different ways. When we use reason to solve a problem, God can speak to us as we work things out. When we are given a spiritual gift to use it means that God contacts us directly – we then act or speak not because we have reasoned something out but because God has enlightened us directly. Clearly our actions then need careful checking, and even the gift of discernment needs thoughtful consideration before it is acted upon.

Discernment is a very important gift for the

Church, and God in his wisdom and love has given this so that the Church will be protected from the evil one; therefore we need to know all we can about this gift and pray that the Church will have discerners and will encourage them.

Obviously, if we do not spend a lot of time listening to what God has said in Scripture and the Church, then it is not likely that we are going to be able to discern his voice when he speaks through other channels. We need to pray for the gift, not necessarily for ourselves, but at least for the body where the gifts operate. We also need to make sure we know what God has already said to us in his Scriptures and in the teachings of the Church. The more we are acquainted with what God has already said, the more we will recognise him as he reveals himself today.

The spiritual gift can be for discerning our own promptings. Is this thought from God or is it just me imagining? For example, I was reading a book the other day in which the author wondered if he was spending too much time talking about God and not enough talking with him. It hit me like a bolt out of the blue. I did not need much discerning – God had spoken forcibly to me.

If, on the other hand, I suddenly get the idea that I ought to open a coffee shop and thus be able to evangelise all sorts of folk that drop in for refreshment, then that needs careful discernment. Was that really God, or was it a bright idea? I need to talk it over with another person and we need to weigh it carefully, using all sorts of human skills. Care must be taken that we are not closed to God. This is not an easy area to discern, and that is why it is always wise to seek another's advice.

We must remember we are not asked to judge the message by whether we like it or not, but rather by whether we sensed God in the manifestation or not. Spiritual gifts require spiritual people to handle them properly and to recognise them.

Honesty and love in any group are of utmost importance. We can be tempted to keep quiet when we feel differently from what others think or say. If while a prophecy is being given, we feel that it is definitely not from God, then we ought to say so even if someone else says the opposite. We can make the excuse to ourselves that we do not want to hurt anyone, or who am I to say such a thing? This is false thinking, for it is not love to let something happen about which we feel unhappy. Far better to risk hurt than allow error to go unchecked.

As with all the other gifts careful teaching is necessary and then people need to be encouraged to offer what they think might be from God. Mistakes will be made, but that is the way we learn with everything. If we never did anything until we were certain that we had it perfect, then very little would ever get done. God majors on forgiving.

People need sound teaching on the gifts, which is not too easy to come by in these days when there is so much suspicion towards them. Encouragement needs to be given for people to step out and share what is in their minds and allow others to give their opinion. In this way love will bind us together and we shall be glad to have others who will talk honestly to us, and allow us to talk honestly to them. None of this is easy, especially as we live in a society that has learnt to be polite and imagine that that is being kind.

REFLECTIONS

- Can you see the difference between the virtue of discernment and the charismatic gift?
- Are you ever aware of your own spirit?
- How would you check an inspiration that came to you either at a prayer-time or outside it?
- Spiritual gifts usually require a certain spiritual maturity in the person in whom they operate. Of course, God can use anyone with his inspirations. Do you expect God ever to use you for discernment?

Baptism in the Holy Spirit

One of the things that worried me most, when I met the Pentecostal Movement, was the baptism in the Holy Spirit. What happened seemed very simple: a group gathered round a person and prayed that Jesus would baptise them with his Spirit. The effect was nearly always visible, either there and then, with the person becoming charged with a deep joy and happiness, or it happened quite soon afterwards. This had me puzzling: why didn't the sacrament of baptism have the same effect?

One could argue that most baptisms involve infants, but I have seen enough adult baptisms to know that there is usually no visible effect for those baptised. Theologically I could not answer the question, nor could I find anyone who gave me a satisfactory explanation. Many warned me that anything 'Pentecostal' was bound to have a lot of emotional exuberance.

While I could not understand what was going on

in this baptism in the Spirit, I certainly could tell from the results that something powerful was happening. God obviously became real for these people; somehow they knew Jesus and not just knew about him, he was real to them; they had an ability to praise God and do it out loud; they could witness boldly before others without embarrassment; they developed a great love for Scripture and would read and refer to it frequently; and often one of the spiritual gifts became active, most commonly, tongues.

I confess I never dared pluck up courage to ask for this baptism in the early days, though I longed for what it seemed to offer. As a priest I felt responsible, and I did not want to lead people into something about which I was not at all certain so I kept myself detached.

Now, some twenty-eight years afterwards, I think I understand what was happening. In the early Church baptism was given to willing adults. They had heard the good news about what Jesus had done for them, and they came willingly to receive all he had won for them – forgiveness for their sins and a new life in him. They came to their baptism with a lively faith, responding to God and his gift.

Today the scene is very different. Usually the one receiving baptism is an infant, so personal faith is absent, though there is faith, hopefully, in the parents and godparents. But even when the person is an adult there can, instead of faith in what Jesus has done, be more of a desire to belong to a Christian family.

Also the spiritual environment today is greatly different from earlier days when, even though infant baptism was practised, the child grew up in an atmosphere of faith. Living in a community of believers greatly strengthens the faith of all, leading the child to understand much better his or her own baptism.

Sacraments are not magic, they need to be given and accepted. Baptism and confirmation confer a supernatural gift, but ignorance or lack of understanding of the gift, can block its full effect. In other words, while the sacrament is valid and has been given, the effect has been blocked. When the block is removed then the full effect floods in.

I believe, through this renewal, many, many people have understood for the first time about the lordship of Jesus Christ and what he has achieved for them at such terrible cost, and they have seen clearly that Christianity is not about doing and then receiving, but rather receiving then doing. Therefore what has come to be called baptism in the Holy Spirit has been an opportunity for awakening in them their sacraments of initiation.

There is vast ignorance among the faithful today. Many have received a very sketchy understanding of their religion. Many have been educated after the Second Vatican Council, when it has not been at all clear what should be taught. While ecumenism is of such great importance, it is not easy to change a dyed-in-the-wool attitude overnight. And now that we are trying to build bridges with those of other faiths, there is considerable confusion among Catholics and Catholic teachers. We need very clear gospel teaching, and I believe the charismatic renewal has been one of the most important stirrings in the Church this century because it has evangelised the baptised.

There is no hard and fast way of receiving baptism in the Holy Spirit. All that is necessary is a real desire to receive what Jesus has achieved for us, but of course, in order to have that desire we need to know what he has achieved for us. The renewal has produced a seminar known as 'Life in the Spirit'.* This provides an ideal opportunity for people to go over the basics of the faith, which many have never done since their school-days.

We can ask another person, or a group, to pray with us for the baptism, or we can simply ask God for it by ourselves. Each year the Church offers us an opportunity to renew our sacramental baptism during the vigil service on Holy Saturday night; and that is what baptism in the Spirit is about. Do not judge the result of the prayer by how you feel. We must learn to live by faith and not by feelings. Feelings are not wrong; they are like the English weather – unreliable.

Jesus told us to ask and we would receive and he also said: 'If you then, who are evil, know how to give your children what is good, how much more will the heavenly Father give the Holy Spirit to those who ask him' (Luke 11:13). Again we have to hang on to the truth that Christianity is about receiving, then doing. We ask because we have need, not because we are worthy.

Because we are constantly learning more and more about God and all he has done for us, it is a good

* Further information about the 'Life in the Spirit' seminar can be obtained from the National Service Committee for Catholic Charismatic Renewal, Allen Hall, 28 Beaufort Street, London SW3 5AA.

practice to accept again and again, quite deliberately, our baptism.

REFLECTIONS

● Have you ever heard the term 'baptised in the Holy Spirit'?
● Have you experienced it, or have you ever suddenly had a second conversion or a clear insight into how much God loves you? It does not really matter what name you give to this experience, it usually means that the initiation sacraments are flowering in you.
● Do you understand that a 'born again' experience does not mean that is the moment you became a Christian, but means that is the moment when you realised the significance of being a Christian?

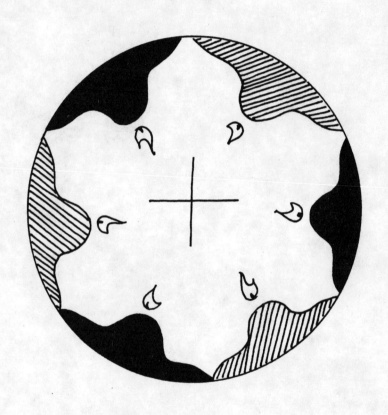

14

Prayer Meetings

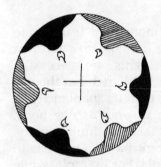

Many people think that the charismatic renewal is all about prayer meetings. But I must emphasise that the prayer meeting is not the essence of the renewal. The renewal is for the whole Church; prayer meetings are not for everyone.

Prayer meetings grew out of renewal. People had caught a new vision of God, and they wanted to praise and bless him, singing songs and canticles. Others who had not experienced this new vision of God, were attracted to these groups and had a new experience of prayer, often far deeper than anything they had experienced in a church service. Naturally they wanted to bring this experience home to their friends, their parish, and so they tried to set up a prayer meeting; but alas, often the initial new vision of God was not there, and it is very hard to praise God if he is not very exciting to you. Where a group of people had caught the new vision, then others coming to their meeting often were taught about this good God, and so they entered into the joy. Prayer meetings became very popular, and they spread like wildfire, but the mistake that was made was prayer meetings were being spread, whereas the good news about the Lord should have been spread. The result has been that many prayer meetings have become quite heavy, and although spontaneous prayer is there, the inspiration is often lacking.

Requires Discipline

A prayer meeting is much more than learning to pray out loud and being able to make up your own prayer. Obviously these elements are necessary, otherwise the prayer will not be shared; but there is far more to a prayer meeting than its spontaneity. A prayer meeting has to learn to pray as one body. That is really difficult to do. Take our human body: it is made up of many different parts, but it has to work in harmony to be a whole. For example, while I am typing this chapter, my legs do not exercise their gift of walking. Too often prayer meetings have become everyone praying out loud what they wish and when they wish. The result has been pretty chaotic. At first individuals may have felt a certain satisfaction in being able to pray out loud and contribute to the meeting; but if no one is really listening nor responding, then it is hardly one body at prayer. It is just a group of individuals praying out loud. Many prayer meetings started this way, but after a time the novelty wore off and they disbanded. Others have grown and developed as a body at prayer.

Let us look at how the Church prays. She gives us some thoughts about God's love for us or about what the Son has done for us, so that we may respond with thanksgiving and praise. In a prayer meeting it is the same; someone shares an insight or better still a Scripture passage, and then the group begins to respond freely to what has been shared. It may inspire someone to read another passage from Scripture related to what has been said; or it may inspire someone to thank God with a spontaneous prayer; another may want to sing a song that relates to what has been said; yet another may say a formal prayer that echoes the thought being shared. This is true spontaneity; it responds to the initial thought or reading shared. This requires discipline; we have to lay down our own ideas if they do not belong to what is happening at that moment. This also checks those who tend to dominate the meeting with their own ideas and thoughts. If the group is not well founded in the gospel and rooted in Jesus Christ, in other words if its members are not soaking themselves in Scripture between the meetings, then there is a risk that the sharing and prayers will be man-centred and not God-centred. Piety can flourish where solid gospel teaching is lacking. As I have said, many Christians need teaching in the foundational truths, and therefore prayer groups do need periods of teaching. Alas, there are not too many people equipped to do that but in time that will be remedied.

Simple a,b,c Rule

A prayer meeting does need a leader, not that he or she has to dominate or run the meeting. Someone is needed to start it off and bring it to an end. Also it is good to have someone who can prompt it when it gets lost or uninspired. A good way to start a prayer meeting is to get everyone to turn away from their concerns and worries by blessing and praising God for what he has done for us through his Son Jesus Christ. This period of praise is important. It can truly be a sacrifice of praise especially when we do not feel like praising. This time of praise should involve everyone. If the group has a good musician, then that is a great blessing because songs of praise involve everyone. There should be opportunities after a song for individuals to praise spontaneously or for the whole group to praise out loud together. Tongues can be used at this point. It takes time for a group to learn how to praise God. It is not done by trying to stir people's emotions, far better to get people to soak their minds in the great events that have brought us new life in Jesus. When the Spirit of God begins to make these events real to us, we will find praise welling up in our hearts. When we praise God we are doing the highest thing a person can do.

Some prayer meetings spend most of the time praising God and only towards the end is there an opportunity for someone to share God's Word through a reading or a prophecy. Other prayer meetings spend ten, fifteen or twenty minutes in praise, then sit to allow sharing of Scripture to happen. This is the time when the body tries to pray as one unit. When someone shares Scripture, then all reflect on what was shared and respond to it in different ways. In this way themes develop, different people give different insights, and the group grows because of each other's openness to God. This forms community, gratitude develops for each other, but our woundedness and selfishness are also brought up. There will be times when we have to confess to each other and ask forgiveness; there will also be times when we may have to confront one member with some fault. This is a time for real growth, and we move from just enjoying being with the group to become a loving community.

Towards the end of the meeting, the leader should, if possible, recap the meeting, pointing out what God seemed to be saying to the group, and then open the prayertime for special requests. This should be reasonably short. I have been at meetings where we have droned on, praying for every conceivable need, all very wearisome and counter-productive. All petitions should be made with hope in the risen living Lord. Finally a simple a,b,c rule can be helpful: a – be audible, b – be brief, c – be Christ-centred.

I have found that liturgical prayer, personal prayer and shared prayer, all nourish each other. Liturgical prayer taught me what personal prayer was about; personal prayer has taught me what shared prayer was about. But prayer without the renewal of one's personal relationship with God can become a blind alley. Prayer is very important, but it must not become an idol. Prayer must not become an end in itself, it must lead me to God, not experiences of God, but to God himself. That leads us to the final question: who is the God we pray to? What is he like? If we are wrong about him, then we will be wrong about everything that has to do with him, even our prayer.

REFLECTIONS

- Do you belong to a prayer group?
- Does spontaneous prayer threaten you? If so why?
- Do you like or dislike prayer meetings? Give reasons for your answer. Remember there are 'many rooms' in the Father's house (John 14:2).
- Do you prefer praying alone? Is that because you can escape the inconvenience of other people? This does not mean private prayer is wrong, it only asks are our motives wrong?

Epilogue

Taking authority, commanding in the Lord's name, acting in the power of the Risen Lord is certainly part of the gospel but it is also very seductive. Power, even if it is the Lord's, can appeal to our rebellious self.

If we have understood Christianity from a rather negative point of view, submitting and letting God have his way, it is very intoxicating to discover that we are sent out, in the power of his Spirit, to continue the work Christ came to do. It is no wonder my priesthood had seemed so powerless for it had never occurred to me to call on the power of the Lord, though of course I knew his power was in the sacraments, but my work involved much more than administering sacraments.

But is this power to be had for the asking? Peter was once delivered from prison, but there was a later time when he was led out and executed. I am sure many prayers were said for his deliverance on both occasions. I am also sure that many prayers went up from concentration camps, and yet the Lord did not intervene. Recently Bosnia and Rwanda have had all the eyes of the world focused on them, and I know many prayers have been said, but there has been no sudden miracle.

We must remember that God's ways are not ours. Today God has made his gifts of power appear again, but they are not for our glory, nor for us to use as we will. Pope Paul VI said of the renewal that 'It was a chance for the Church' and the present Pope has said:

The emergence of the Renewal following the Second Vatican Council was a particular gift of the Holy Spirit to the Church. It was a sign of a desire on the part of many Catholics to live more fully their Baptismal dignity and vocation as adopted sons and daughters of the Father, to know the redeeming power of Christ our Saviour in a more intense experience of individual and group prayer, and to follow the teachings of the Scriptures by reading them in the light of the same Spirit who inspired their writing. Certainly one of the most important results of this spiritual reawakening has been the increased thirst for holiness which is seen in the lives of individuals and in the whole Church.